The Great Within

The Great Within

by

Christian D. Larson

A NEWCASTLE CLASSIC

NEWCASTLE PUBLISHING CO., INC.
NORTH HOLLYWOOD, CALIFORNIA

Originally published in 1912 by L.N. Fowler & Co. of London, and The New Literature Publishing Company of Los Angeles.

ISBN: 0-87877-237-5
A Newcastle Classic
First printing 1996
10 9 8 7 6 5 4 3 2 1
Printed in the United States of America.

The Great Within

The Great Within

THE mind of man is conscious and subconscious, objective and subjective, external and internal.

The conscious mind acts, the subconscious reacts; the conscious mind produces the impression, the subconscious produces the expression; the conscious mind determines what is to be done, the subconscious supplies the mental material and the necessary power.

The subconscious mind is the great within—an inner mental world from which all things proceed that appear in the being of man.

The conscious mind is the mind of action, the subconscious mind is the mind of reaction, but every subconscious reaction is invariably the direct result of a corresponding conscious action.

Every conscious action produces an impression upon the subconscious and every subconscious reaction produces an expression in the personality.

Everything that is expressed through the personality was first impressed upon the subconscious, and since the conscious mind may impress anything upon the subconscious, any desired expression may be secured, because the subconscious will invariably do what it is directed and impressed to do.

The subconscious mind is a rich mental field; every conscious impression is a seed sown in this field, and will bear fruit after its kind, be the seed good or otherwise.

All thoughts of conviction and all deeply felt desires will impress themselves upon the subconscious and will reproduce their kind, to be later expressed in the personal being of man.

Every desire for power, ability, wisdom, harmony, joy, health, purity, life, greatness, will impress itself upon the subconscious, and will cause the thing desired to be produced in the great within, the quality and the quantity depending upon the depth of the desire and the conscious realization of the true idea conveyed by the desire.

What is produced in the within will invariably come forth into expression in the personality; therefore, by knowing how to impress the subconscious, man may give his personal self any quality desired, and in any quantity desired.

Personal power, physical health, mental brilliancy, remarkable ability, extraordinary talent, rare genius—these are attainments that the subconscious of every mind can readily produce and bring forth when properly directed and impressed.

The subconscious mind obeys absolutely the desires of the conscious mind, and since the subconscious is limitless, it can do for man whatever he may desire to have done.

What man may desire to become, that he can become, and the art of directing and impressing the subconscious is the secret.

Unlimited possibilities do exist in the subconscious of every mind, and since these possibilities can all be developed, there is no end to the attainments and achievements of man.

Nothing is impossible; the great within is limitless—the inexhaustible source of everything that may be required for the highest development and the greatest accomplishments in human life, and whatever we may direct the within to produce, the same will invariably be produced.

T properly direct and impress the subconscious, the first essential is to realize that the subconscious mind is a finer mentality that permeates every fibre of the entire personality. Though the subconscious can be impressed most directly through the brain-center, the volume of subconscious expression will increase in proportion to our conscious realization of subconscious life in every part of mind and body.

To concentrate attention frequently upon the subconscious side of the entire personality will steadily awaken the great within; this will cause one to feel that a new and superior being is beginning to unfold, and with that feeling comes the conviction that unbounded power does exist in the deeper life of man.

When the awakening of the subconscious is felt in every part of mind and body, one knows that anything may be attained and achieved; doubts disappear absolutely, because to feel the limitless is to believe in the limitless.

While impressing the subconscious, attention should be directed upon the inside of mind, and this is readily done while one *thinks* that the subconscious mentality permeates the personality, as water permeates a sponge.

Think of the interior essence that permeates the exterior substance, and cause all mental actions to move toward the finer mental life that lives and moves and has its being within the interior mind. This will cause the conscious action to impress itself directly upon the subconscious, and a corresponding reaction or expression will invariably follow.

While directing attention upon the subconscious, the idea that is to be impressed should be clearly discerned in mind and an effort should be made to feel the soul of that idea.

To mentally feel the soul of the idea will completely eliminate the mechanical tendency of mental action, and this is extremely important because no mechanical action of mind can impress the subconscious.

Perfect faith in the process is indispensable, and to inwardly know that results will be secured is to cause failure to become impossible.

The deeper and higher the attitude of faith while the subconscious is being impressed, the more deeply will the impression be made, and the deep impression not only enters the richest states of the subconscious, but always produces results.

The attitude of faith takes the mind into the superior, the limitless, the soul of things, and this is precisely what is wanted.

When the mind transcends the objective it enters into the subjective, and to enter into the subjective is to impress one's ideas and desires directly, deeply and completely upon the great within. Such impressions will invariably produce remarkable expressions, not only because they have entered more deeply into the subconscious, but also because every impression that is made in the attitude of faith is given superior quality, greater power and higher worth.

The subconscious should never be approached in the attitude of command or demand, but always in the attitude of faith and desire. Never command the subconscious to do thus or so, but desire with a deep, strong desire, that the subconscious do what you desire to have done, and animate that desire with the faith that it positively will be done.

To combine a high faith with a strong desire while impressing the subconscious is the secret through which results may invariably be secured.

The subconscious should never be forcefully aroused, but should be gradually awakened and developed through such actions of mind as are deep and strong while perfectly serene.

Deep thoughts on all important subjects, lofty aspirations on all occasions, and a constantly expanding consciousness will aid remarkably in awakening the great within.

Whenever attention is directed upon the subconscious, an effort should be made to expand consciousness by picturing upon mind the expanding process while the deeper feeling of thought is placing itself in touch with the universal; a strong, deep desire for greater things should be impressed upon the inner mentality, and a deep stillness should animate every action of mind.

The inner side of mind should always be acted upon peacefully, though not with that peacefulness that has a tendency to produce inaction, but with that peacefulness that produces a high, strong action that continues to act in serenity and poise.

To concentrate a strong, deeply felt, well poised mental action upon the entire subconscious mentality a number of times every day will, in a remarkably short time, develop the great within to such an extent that the mind will inwardly know that unlimited power and innumerable possibilities have been placed at its command, and when this realization comes the mind may go on to any attainment and any achievement; failure will be simply impossible.

When the development of the subconscious has been promoted to a degree the conscious mind will instinctively feel that failure is impossible, and will, consequently, leave results to the law. There will be no anxiety about results because to feel the presence of subconscious action is to know that results must follow when the subconscious is properly directed and impressed.

Perfect faith in the law that the subconscious will invariably do whatever it is impressed to do will eliminate anxiety completely, and this is extremely important, because the subconscious mind cannot proceed to do what it has been impressed to do so long as there is anxiety in the conscious mind.

Provide the proper conditions and the law will positively produce the desired results, and to inwardly know this is the first essential in providing the proper conditions.

The subconscious mind is somewhat similar to the phonograph; under certain conditions it can record anything, and under certain other conditions it can reproduce everything that has been recorded. There is this difference, however: The subconscious not only reproduces exactly what has been recorded, but will also form, create, develop and express what mind may desire when the impression is being made; that is, the subconscious not only reproduces the seed itself, but as many more seeds as the original seed desired to reproduce, and also the exact degree of improvement in quality that was latent in the desire of the original seed or impression.

The subconscious not only reproduces the mental idea contained in the impression, but also every essential that may be required to fulfill the desire of that impression.

Through this law the subconscious can find the answer to any question or work out any problem when properly impressed with an exact idea of what is wanted.

HE subconscious provides the essentials, but the conscious mind must apply those essentials before practical results may be secured.

When the subconscious is directed to produce health, those mental actions will be expressed that can produce health in the body when combined with normal physical actions, and it is the conscious mind that must produce the normal physical actions; that is, common sense living.

When the subconscious is directed to produce success, those elements, qualities and powers will be expressed in mind and body that can, if consciously applied, produce success.

That the subconscious can do anything is absolutely true, but it is true in this sense, that it can supply the power, the capacity and the understanding to do anything, but the conscious mind must practically apply what the subconscious has brought forth into expression.

The subconscious supplies the power and the mental elements, but these must be used by the conscious mind if the desired results are to be secured. Nothing comes ready-made from the subconscious, but it can give us the material from which we can make anything.

The subconscious can give you the powers and qualities of genius, and if you apply, practically and constantly, those powers and qualities, you will become a genius.

The subconscious can give you the life and the power that is necessary to remarkable talents, and if you use that life and power in the daily cultivation of your talents, those talents will become remarkable.

The law is that the conscious mind must impress its desires upon the subconscious in order to secure the mental essentials that may be required to fulfill those desires, but the conscious mind must *use* those essentials before results can be secured.

It is the conscious mind that does things, but it is the subconscious that supplies the power with which those things are done, and by learning to draw upon the subconscious the conscious mind can do anything, because unbounded power and innumerable possibilities are latent in the great within.

The proper conditions for recording an impression upon the subconscious are deep feeling, strong desires, conscious interest and a living faith. When these are blended harmoniously in the conscious actions of mind the subconscious will be directed and impressed properly and the desired response will invariably appear.

The principal essential, however, is deep feeling; no idea or desire can enter the subconscious unless it is deeply felt, and every idea or desire that is deeply felt will enter the subconscious of itself, whether or not we desire to have it do so.

It is through this law that man is affected by his environments, surroundings and external conditions, because whenever he permits himself to be deeply impressed by that with which he may come in contact those impressions will enter the subconscious.

What enters the subconscious of any mind will become a part of that mind, and will, to a degree, affect the nature, the character, the quality, the thoughts and the actions of that mind.

When the subconscious is impressed by external conditions the impressions will be like those conditions and, as like produces like, conditions will be produced in the subconscious that are exactly like those external conditions from which the impressions came.

The individual, therefore, who permits his subconscious to be indiscriminately impressed by external conditions will think and act, more or less, as his environments may suggest. In many respects his life will be controlled completely by those persons and things with which he may come in contact, while in nearly all other respects his life will be greatly modified by the presence of those persons and things.

The mind that does not control its feelings may be subconsciously impressed by any external action, be that action good or otherwise, while the mind that can give deep feeling to any idea can impress any idea upon the subconscious, and as the whole of the individual life is determined by what the subconscious is directed or impressed to do, the former will become, more or less, like his environment, having control neither of himself nor his destiny; the latter, however, may become what he wants to become and will master both himself and his destiny.

No undesirable feeling should ever be permitted; no wrong idea should ever be given in thought; nor should one ever think seriously, feelingly or sympathetically about wrong or evil in any shape or form.

To think feelingly about wrong is to impress wrong upon the subconscious; it is to sow undesirable seeds in the garden of the mind, and a harvest of weeds—sickness, trouble and want, will be the result.

Good thoughts, deeply felt, will bring health, happiness, harmony, peace, power, ability and character. Wrong thoughts, deeply felt, will bring discord, depression, fear, sickness, weakness and failure.

To properly impress the subconscious at all times, it is therefore necessary to train the mind to think only of those things that one desires to realize and express in tangible life; and what one does not wish to meet in personal experience should never be given a single moment of thought.

What we mentally feel we invariably impress upon the subconscious, and there is a tendency to mentally feel every thought that is given prolonged or serious attention.

To think about that which we do not want, is to impress upon the subconscious what we do not wish to impress; and as every impression produces a corresponding expression, we will thereby receive the very things we desire to avoid.

It is through this law that what we fear always comes upon us, because what we fear will impress itself upon the subconscious without fail.

To fear disease, failure or trouble is to sow seeds in the subconscious field that will bring forth a harvest of diseased conditions, troubled thoughts, confused mental states and misdirected actions in mind and body.

The more intense the fear the deeper the subconscious impression, and the more we shall receive of that which we feared we should receive.

Through the same law we always receive what we continue to expect in the desire of the deep, strong faith. The more faith we have in the realization and attainment of that which has quality, superiority and worth, the more deeply we impress the subconscious with those mental seeds that can and will bring forth the greater good that we desire.

To have faith in the attainment of peace, harmony, health, power, ability, talent and genius, while directing the subconscious to produce those things, is to cause those very things to be created within us in greater and greater measure.

THE purpose of consciously and intelligently directing the subconscious is first, to correct every wrong, every flaw, every defect, every perversion, and every imperfect condition that may exist in the personality of man; and, second, to bring out into fuller expression the limitless possibilities that exist in the great within.

Everything that is wrong in the personal life of the individual comes from a corresponding wrong impression in the subconscious; the wrong subconscious impression is the cause, the wrong external condition is the effect; it is therefore evident that to remove all wrong impressions from the subconscious is to establish complete emancipation throughout the entire personal being of man.

To remove any wrong impression from the subconscious, the opposite correct impression must be made in its place. A wrong impression cannot be removed by mental force, resistance or denial; produce the right impression and the wrong impression will cease to exist.

By training the mind to think only of that which is desired in actual realization and experience, and by deeply impressing all those thoughts and desires upon the subconscious, every undesirable impression will be removed; the cause of every flaw, defect or perversion in the personal man will be removed, and in consequence, the flaws, defects, and perversions themselves will cease to exist.

The entire subconscious field can be changed absolutely by constantly causing new and superior impressions to be formed in the great within; and every change that is brought about in the subconscious will produce a corresponding change in mind and body.

There is nothing adverse in the mentality or the personality of man that cannot be corrected by causing the correct impression to be formed in the subconscious. All wrongs, flaws or defects, whether they be hereditary, or personally produced, can be removed completely through the intelligent direction of the subconscious.

Every impression that is properly made in the subconscious mind will produce a corresponding expression in the personality; that is the law, and it cannot fail; but the impression must be properly made.

The subconscious does not respond to mere commands, because it neither reasons nor discriminates; it does not obey what it is told to do, but what it is impressed to do. It is the idea that enters into the subconscious that determines subconsclous action; but the idea must not simply be given to the subconscious, it must *enter into* the subconscious.

The idea that predominates in mind while the subconscious is being directed, is the idea that will be impressed; therefore, negative desires will impress the subconscious to do the very opposite to what is desired by the desire.

To direct the subconscious to remove sickness is to impress the idea of sickness, because the mind thinks principally of sickness at the time; in consequence, more sickness will be produced.

It is not what the subconscious is directed to do, but the predominant thought that is conveyed through that direction that determines results; therefore, the predominant thought must be identical with the final results desired.

When health is desired, no thought whatever should be given to sickness; the subconscious should not be directed to remove sickness, but should be directed to *produce* health.

The subconscious should always be directed to produce those qualities and conditions that are desired, but those conditions that are to be removed should never be mentioned in mind. Adverse conditions will disappear of themselves when true conditions are established; but the mind cannot impress, create and establish the true while attention is being concentrated upon the adverse.

To direct the subconscious not to do thus or so, is to impress the subconscious to do that very thing. When you try to impress the subconscious with the idea that you do not wish to get sick any more you have sickness in mind, and it is the idea that you have in mind that you impress upon the subconscious.

To remove sickness forget sickness absolutely, and impress upon the subconscious the idea of health, and that idea alone. Desire health with all the power of mind, and fill both sides of mentality, conscious and subconscious, so completely with that desire that every thought of sickness is forgotten.

A denial will impress upon the subconscious the nature and the power of the very thing that is denied; therefore, to deny evil or resist evil is to produce causes in mind that will, in the coming days, produce more evil.

To try to deny away adverse conditions is to continue in perpetual mental warfare with those very things that mind is trying to destroy. Temporary states of seeming freedom in some parts of the system will be followed regularly with outbreaks of adversity in other parts; while the subconscious cause of undesirable conditions in mind or body will not be removed.

So long as we continue to resist or deny evil, we will think about evil, and so long as we think about evil, evil will be impressed upon the subconscious; and whatever we impress upon the subconscious, that the subconscious will reproduce and bring forth into the personal life.

When we have a great undertaking that we wish to promote, and desire to secure as much added power, ability and capacity as possible from the great within, the subconscious should not be directed to prevent failure. To think of failure is to impress, the subconscious with the idea of failure, and detrimental conditions—conditions that will confuse the mind and produce failure—will be expressed.

All thought of failure should be eliminated, and the subconscious should be deeply impressed to produce success. The subconscious will respond by bringing forth the power, the capacity, the ability, the understanding and the determination that can and will produce success.

HEN properly directed, the subconscious mind can inspire the conscious mind to do the right thing at the right time, to take advantage of opportunities during the psychological moment, and to so deal with circumstances that all things will work together to promote the object in view. It is, therefore, evident that when the subconscious is trained to work in harmony with the objects and desires of the conscious mind, failure becomes impossible, and success in greater and greater measures may be secured by anyone.

When trying to remove undesirable habits, tendencies or desires, the mind should never think, "I shall not do this any more," because through such a thought or statement, the habit in mind will be reimpressed upon the subconscious and will gain a deeper foothold in the system than it had before.

The proper course to pursue is to forget completely what you desire to remove; refuse to think of it; when tempted to think of the matter turn attention upon the opposite qualities, desires or tendencies. Should you fail to become sufficiently interested in those opposite desires to forget what you want to forget, look for the most interesting points of view connected with those desires. The mental effort employed in trying to find the most interesting point of view connected with those desires will cause the mind to become thoroughly interested in those desires, and will, consequently, forget those things that should be forgotten.

While the mind is being interested in those desires that you wish to cultivate, they should be impressed upon the subconscious with all the depth of feeling that can possibly be aroused. These impressions should be repeated a number of times every day, and the new desires will soon take root in the subconscious.

Every desire or tendency that takes root in the subconscious will begin to develop and express itself in the personal self, and will be felt throughout the personality. When the new desire is fully expressed, it will be thoroughly felt; and since no two desires of opposite nature can exist in the person at the same time, the old desires will disappear; the old tendencies and the old habits will have vanished completely.

To impress upon the subconscious a strong desire for the better, the purer and the superior, is to cause the system to crave something better; the force of desire will be refined; the entire organism will be purified, and the wants of the personal self will become normal on a higher plane.

All kinds of undesirable habits may be removed by constantly impressing upon the subconscious the idea of pure desire; and all tendencies to anger, hatred and similar states, may be removed by causing the qualities of love, kindness, justice and sympathy to be more fully developed in the great within.

To remove fear and worry, impress the subconscious, as frequently as possible, with the deep feeling of faith, gratitude and mental sunshine.

To have faith is to know that man has the power to perpetually increase the good, and that he may constantly press on to better things and greater things. To have faith is to be guided by superior mental lucidity, and thereby know how to select what is safe and secure; and he who knows that he is on the safe path, the ascending path, the endless path to better things and greater things, has eliminated fear absolutely.

To live constantly in the spirit of gratitude is not only to remove worry, but the cause of worry. To be grateful for the good that is now coming into life is to open the way for the coming of greater good. This is the law; and he who is daily receiving the greater good, has no cause for worry; he will even forget that worry ever had a place in his mind.

To constantly impress the subconscious with mental sunshine, is to establish the tendency to live on the bright side, the sunny side; and to live on the brlght side is to increase your own brightness; your mind will become more brilliant, your thinking will have more lucidity and clearness, your nature will have more sweetness, your personality will be in more perfect harmony with everything, your life will be better, your work will be better—everything will be better; therefore, by living on the bright side, all things will steadily become better and brighter for you.

When all is dark, and everything seems to go wrong, arouse all your energies for the purpose of impressing and directing the subconscious to produce the change you desire. Give the deepest possible feeling to those impressions, and have stronger faith than you ever had before.

Continue persistently until the great within begins to respond; you will then feel from within how to act, and you will be given the power to do what you feel you should do. Ere long, things will take a turn; the threatened calamity will be avoided by the coming forth of that power within that is greater than all adversities, all troubles, all wrongs; and instead, this power, having been awakened, will proceed to create a better future than you ever knew before.

WHILE the subconscious is being impressed, no thought whatever should be given to limitation, and no comparisons should be made with other persons or previous attainments.

To think that you wish to do better to-day than you did yesterday, is to give the subconscious two unrelated ideas upon which to act—the idea of the lesser achievement of the past and the idea of the greater achievement of the future. The subconscious will try to reproduce them both, but as they are antagonistic, they will neutralize each other, and there will be no results. The greater and the lesser cannot be produced by the same force at the same time.

To impress the desire that you may become greater than anyone else, will also present to the subconscious two conflicting ideas; and the results again will be neutralized.

The course to pursue is to forget the lesser achievements of yesterday; think only of the greater achievements that you wish to promote to-day; then direct the subconscious to do to-day what you wish to have done to-day. This will cause the great within to give all its power and attention to the one idea—the greater achievement of to-day; and the greater achievement will positively follow.

Know what you desire to become; resolve to become what you desire to become, whether others have reached those heights or not; forget the lesser heights that others have reached and give your whole mind and soul to the greater heights that you have resolved to reach.

You can become what you desire to become; the great within is limitless, and can give you all the wisdom and all the power that you may require. Knowing this, direct the great within to bring forth what you may need to reach your lofty goal, and the same will be done. The subconscious never fails to do what it is properly directed to do.

While impressing the subconscious, think of the perfect in regard to quality, and the limitless in regard to quantity. Never specify any exact amount, nor any special degree; always desire the limitless and the perfect; desire nothing less; and animate consciousness with a strong desire to expand constantly during the process, so that the highest quality and the greatest quantity possible may be realized.

Desire the fullest possible expression in the great eternal now; realize that your own inherent powers and capabilities are limitless, and impress that idea upon the subconscious.

Give no thought whatever to the lesser attainments in your own life or in the lives of others, but keep your mental eye single upon what you wish to become, knowing that you can become what you wish to become because there are no limitations in the great within.

When the subconscious begins to respond, a distinct sensation is frequently felt of some interior power working through you; this means that greater power from within is being awakened, and the outer mind should give full right of way so that a complete expression may be secured; that is, the conscious mind should become quiet, serene and thoroughly receptive, and should forget the personal self, for the time.

When the personal self is forgotten and the greater interior self is given full possession of both the mentality and the personality—it is then that one's greatest work is done. It is then that real ability, real talent and real genius can appear in tangible life and action.

When the musician forgets herself, there is something in her music that awakens the very depths of the soul, and you are lifted to a fairer world than you ever knew before.

When the artist forgets himself, his pictures are given immortal life and every touch reveals a universe of indescribable beauty.

When the orator forgets himself, he speaks as one having authority, and you inwardly feel that every word is true.

When the practical man of affairs forgets himself, he is given a power that is irresistible, and the obstacles that are encountered in the way, disappear as if they never had the slightest existence.

It is such people that do great things in the world; it is such people who live in the human heart after ages have passed away; and their secret is this—the greatness within them was awakened, and was permitted to give full expression to its rare and superior power.

When you feel this higher power mysteriously moving within the greater depths of mind and soul, you know what is taking place; be calm, and give the superior self the right of way.

At first this power may feel as if it were distinct from yourself; but it is not, it is your own superior power; the coming forth of your own limitless power; the very power that you have for some time been directing the subconscious to produce; and when you *feel* that it is your own it is placed in your full conscious possession, and will do whatever you may desire or direct.

To inwardly feel that the entire within is your own is extremely important, because the more completely the conscious mind is united with the power of the subconscious, the more perfectly can the conscious mind impress the subconscious, and the more thoroughly can the greater power of the subconscious express itself in external, tangible action.

When you are about to do something that demands the best that is within you, impress the subconscious for higher power; then wait a few moments for this power to appear; and when it does appear, let the outer self obey. The great within has come forth to do your work, and no power in existence can do it better.

To enter into full conscious possession of the higher power from within, and to give full right of way to this power, is to give your objective talents and faculties the greatest power and the best power at your command.

O impress the subconscious for more power it is necessary to give to that impression all the power that mind is conscious of now; in other words, the seed that is already at hand should be placed in rich soil; the power that is now active in the conscious mind should be caused to act upon the subconscious; there will be increase; and by reimpressing the added power upon the subconscious every time added power is gained, this increase will become perpetual.

To proceed, concentrate attention upon the subconscious side of the entire personality, and desire gently, but with deep feeling, to draw all the present active energies of the system into the subconscious.

The more energy that is drawn into the subconscious during this process, the more power will be impressed upon the subconscious, and the more power that is impressed upon the subconscious the more power will be expressed from the subconscious.

The law is that whatever power is impressed upon the subconscious will return to the outer personality with added power, just as every seed sown in rich soil will reproduce itself, ten, twenty, sixty and even a hundredfold.

Therefore, to daily arouse all the power that we personally possess, and to impress all of that power upon the subconscious, is to increase perpetually the quantity of personal power; and the quality of that power can be steadily improved by transmuting and refining all the present forces of the system before they are impressed upon the subconscious.

Before the conscious mind begins to act upon the subconscious all thought and all feeling should be elevated into the highest states of quality, worth and superiority that can possibly be realized. This will cause the impression to be superior, and a superior impression will produce a superior expression.

That which is common, ordinary or inferior should never be held in mind, nor deeply felt for a moment, because to feel the ordinary is to impress the ordinary upon the subconscious; it is sowing inferior seed, and the harvest will be cheap, common, worthless.

No person should ever think of himself as inferior, or permit himself to recognize the imperfect in his nature. To recognize or feel the imperfect is to sow more seeds of imperfection, and reap another harvest that is not worth while.

There is a superior nature within man; this nature alone should be recognized and felt; only those thoughts and ideas that are formed in the exact likeness of the superior should be impressed upon the subconscious, and the subconscious will respond by giving superiority to the entire mentality and the entire personality.

The average person fails to improve because he lives mainly in the consciousness of his imperfections; he feels that he is ordinary and constantly impresses the subconscious with this feeling of the ordinary; the subconscious naturally responds by producing the ordinary, both in mind and body.

That person, however, who lives in the ideal, who thinks constantly of the greater worth that is within him, and who tries to feel and realize his superior nature, will give quality to every impression that may enter the subconscious; and according to the law of action and reaction, will steadily develop greater quality and worth throughout his entire nature.

The quality of the impression that is given to the subconscious always corresponds with the degree of quality of which we are conscious at the time the impression is made. To refine, elevate and enrich all thought and feeling before the conscious mind begins to act upon the subconscious, is therefore of the highest importance.

The more quality that is given to the power that is being developed, the greater the results that may be secured through the application of that power.

It is quality and quantity combined that produces greatness, and greatness—greater and greater greatness, is the purpose we all have in view.

To constantly feel the greatness of the great within, is to constantly impress upon the subconscious the idea of greatness; this will cause the subconscious to develop greatness and express greatness through every part of the personal man.

As greatness develops, the feeling of greatness will become deeper, stronger and more intense; this will cause larger and finer ideas of greatness to be impressed upon the subconscious; and the result of these later impressions will be larger and greater expressions; a larger measure of greatness will be developed perpetually through the law of much gathering more, or "to him that hath shall be given."

All development comes from the subconscious, and since the possibilities of the great within are limitless, anyone can, through the proper direction of the subconscious, develop remarkable ability, extraordinary talent and rare genius.

All genius is the result of a large subconscious mentality; therefore, any one can become a genius by awakening a larger and a larger measure of the great within.

That a genius is asleep in the subconscious of every mind is literally true, but to awaken this genius is not the only essential; the conscious mind must be cultivated scientifically, so that the superior ability from within may find free and full expression.

The conscious mind should be cultivated, the subconscious should be developed; the conscious mind should be trained to do things, while the subconscious should be directed to give more and more power for the doing of greater and greater things.

The subconscious has the capacity to produce genius in any mind—the greatest genius imaginable, but the conscious mind must be highly cultivated so as to become a fit instrument through which great genius may find expression for its superior work.

When quality and worth are received from the subconscious, the conscious mind should use those things in practical action, so that the outer elements and forces of mind may be trained to appreciate quality and appropriate worth in all their tangible expressions.

The conscious and the subconscious sides

of mind should be placed in the most perfect harmonious relations, so that every impression of the conscious mind may enter deeply into the subconscious and every expression from the subconscious may work through the conscious mind without any restriction or interference whatever.

The entire mind develops through the attainment of deeper and higher states of consciousness of the great within; and as this interior realm is boundless, there is no end to the possibilities of mental development.

To gain this interior consciousness, objective consciousness should be constantly deepened toward the unfathomable within, and this is accomplished by training all the mental tendencies to move toward the within.

The mental tendencies will move toward those states of being to which we give the greatest amount of attention; therefore, by constantly *thinking with deep feeling* of the great within, all the mental tendencies will move toward, and into, the great within; and will carry into the subconscious every idea, thought or desire that the conscious mind may wish to realize and fulfill.

When all the mental tendencies move into the subconscious, and all thought is given feeling, worth and quality, the subconscious will constantly be impressed with superior ideas, which means a constant expression of superior life, superior ability and superior power.

The more deeply the tendencies of mind enter the subconscious, the more of the great within will be awakened; and whatever is awakened in the within will invariably come forth into the personal man.

It is therefore evident that when we cease to live on the surface of personal life we shall constantly improve that surface; by mentally living in the within we shall strengthen, enrich and perfect the without; that is, we improve external effects by going more deeply into the subconscious and increasing the quality and the power of internal causes.

The person who actually enters the deeper life to live will not ignore the body; those who simply dream of inner states of life may neglect the body, but those who thoroughly develop the greater, inner life will become able to give the body the best that can be secured; and they will enjoy physical existence infinitely more than those who simply live on the surface.

It is the truth that whatever we awaken and develop in the great within will invariably come forth into tangible, personal expression.

ACH person is, no more and no less, than what has been given to him by his subconscious mind; and as the subconscious is prepared to give as much as any one may desire, the statement that we all may become whatsoever we may wish to become, is therefore absolutely true; but what the subconscious is to give to any person depends largely upon the movement of his mental tendencies.

All the creative energies of the system follow the tendencies of the mind; therefore, when all the mental tendencies move toward the subconscious, all the surplus energy that is generated in the system will enter the subconscious; and the more energy that enters the subconscious the more of the subconscious will be awakened and developed.

The larger the field that is placed under cultivation the greater the harvest.

Every mental tendency that is trained to enter the subconscious will cause a corresponding tendency to be permanently expressed; therefore, by causing all the worthy tendencies to move toward the subconscious, the subconscious will respond by expressing through the personality the tendencies to be just, true, honest, virtuous, kind, sympathetic, sweet-tempered, cheerful, fearless, faithful, persevering, industrious—in brief, everything that goes to make a strong and worthy personality.

By a simple system of subconscious training, any one can build up the strongest and most beautiful character imaginable, and in a reasonable time make it a permanent part of himself.

A lack of character is due wholly to the fact that the subconscious has been improperly impressed; misleading tendencies have been formed, and let it be remembered that nothing can tempt man to go wrong except the perverse tendencies that are expressed from his own subconscious mind.

Every weak place in mind or character is caused by a subconscious tendency that is going wrong; such tendencies may have been inherited—many of them are, but they can all be corrected by daily directing the subconscious to produce the opposite quality.

To think, with conviction, that human nature is weak, is to impress upon the subconscious the idea of weakness, and the subconscious will respond by producing a tendency to weakness. Therefore, he who thinks he is weak will cause his nature to continue to be weak. We are weak or strong according to what we direct the subconscious to produce in us.

To realize that the great within contains the power to make the personality as strong as we may wish it to be, and to impress upon the subconscious a strong desire for that power, is to direct the subconscious to make us strong; and whatever we direct the subconscious to do, the same will invariably be done.

There is no reason whatever why any person should continue to have a weak body, a weak character or a weak mind; anything in the being of man can be made strong if the subconscious is properly directed to bring forth the greater life and the greater power.

When the great within is awakened we have the powerful personality, the giant mind, the irresistible character and the great soul. The natural result is a great life—a life that is too strong to be tempted, too strong to be swayed or disturbed by adversity, too strong to be turned from the path to its lofty goal. Such a life will not only live a life that *is* life, but will be an endless inspiration to the race; and such a life is waiting in the great within of every soul.

THE great within is the source of all inspirations, all real music, all permanent art, all poetry with soul, all rich thought, all ideas of genuine worth, all invention, all discovery, all science, and the truth that is absolute.

Everything that has worth, be it in a small degree, or in a very great degree, comes directly from the richness of the subconscious; therefore, to do the greater, the mind should enter into the closest touch with the great within, and should expect the very best that the limitless within can produce.

When in need of ideas, plans, methods, ways and means, call upon the subconscious; the call will not be in vain; the subconscious can supply every need, and will invariably do so when properly directed.

While directing the subconscious, however, all conscious action must be in absolute poise; it is not only necessary to impress what we desire but to impress that desire in such a way that it will actually produce an impression.

When in the presence of the great fact that the within is limitless, the mind will naturally become enthusiastic; feeling will run high and is very liable to become over-wrought; but such a feeling has no depth, it is simply superficial emotionalism; it will waste any amount of energy, but will never produce a single impression upon the subconscious.

To impress the subconscious, the mind must be calm, the entire personality must be in poise, and this feeling of poise must have that great depth that touches the very soul of life itself.

Not the slightest trace of emotional enthusiasm must be permitted, nor must feeling run toward the surface at any time; the actions of mind, especially those of feeling, must move toward the great within if the subconscious is to be reached.

There must be no anxiety connected with the desire to impress the subconscious, and every form of doubt must be eliminated completely.

To properly impress the subconscious, faithful application is necessary; also constant practice, and a perseverance that will not give up; but the prize is worthy of the effort.

To realize that the subconscious can, and will, do anything when properly impressed, is to persevere until the proper impression has been made; and it is those who work in this realization that secure the marvelous results.

To eliminate the tendency to feel emotional while acting upon the subconscious, cultivate the substantial feeling; train yourself to *feel* substantial at all times, and wild, empty, overwrought feelings will entirely disappear.

It is the proper feeling that determines the proper impression; the attainment of the deep, substantial feeling is therefore extremely important, though it is equally important to be able to feel the vibrations of the finer forces of the system.

It is the finer forces that impress the subconscious and the subconscious is invariably impressed whenever these forces are felt.

To develop the consciousness of the finer forces, attention should be frequently concentrated upon that life that permeates the tangible elements in every part of being; and during this concentration the feeling of consciousness should be deepened and expanded as much as possible.

Every conscious action should be trained to penetrate to the very depth of life, and during this process the mind should act in the realization that the more deeply it penetrates any element in the personality, the finer will be the forces into which consciousness will enter.

To awaken or arouse any force or element, attention should be concentrated upon that state in which the desired force or element is known to exist, and the mind should *think* of the nature of that force or element according to the best possible understanding that can be formed of that nature.

The same method may be employed in the development of the subconscious side of any desired faculty or talent.

The creative energies of the system always build up those qualities of which the mind may be thinking; therefore, to actually and continually think of the real nature of a great talent is to develop that talent into the same degree of greatness that is discerned in mind.

The power of this method in the development of ability, talent and genius is practically unlimited, because the mind is capable of discerning higher and higher degrees of greatness, and the subconscious is capable of providing creative energies of as high a state of fineness and power as may be required.

To secure the best results from any method through which the great within is to be unfolded and expressed, it is extremely important to use properly the conscious and the subconscious factors of mind at the various stages of the process.

While impressing the subconscious, the conscious mind should be strong, firm, positive and highly active, but should become perfectly quiet and receptive while expecting a response from the subconscious.

Harmony, serenity and poise are indispensable states both when the impression is being made and when the expression is expected.

The right use of the will is of extraordinary importance; and neither time nor effort should be spared in establishing this right use, because where the will is misapplied the subconscious expressions are interfered with to such an extent that results are completely neutralized.

While the subconscious is being impressed, the will should act firmly and directly upon that consciousness that is felt in the subconscious, but when the subconscious is expected to respond the will should be relaxed into a state of complete inaction.

It is not the purpose of the will to control the outer person by acting directly upon the outer person; the will controls the outer person by causing the subconscious to produce in the outer person whatever may be desired; but when the subconscious begins to express what the will has desired and directed, the will must, for the time being, cease to act.

The true function of the will is to act upon the finer states of consciousness; that is, the subconscious states, those states that are felt in the deeper life of the personality or the mentality; and while in such action, to impress upon the subconscious those causes that can produce the desired effects.

When these causes have been impressed, and the time has come for the expected results, the will must withdraw so that the personality may become sufficiently receptive to give the subconscious response the fullest and freest possible expression.

The subconscious expression will come of itself, at the time designated, if the impression has been properly made; but every attempt of the will to help draw forth that expression will interfere with results.

When the desired subconscious expression fails to appear at the time designated, the impression has either not been properly made, or the subconscious response is being prevented by too much active will force, anxiety or objective commotion.

The subconscious cannot express itself, or do what it is directed to do unless the outer mentality and personality are in poise; but perfect poise is not possible so long as will power is applied upon the external side of mind or body.

Train the will to act upon the subconscious, and the subconscious only, and this is readily accomplished by always turning attention upon the subconscious whenever the will is being employed.

When acting upon the objective, the will only interferes with normal functions, and can accomplish absolutely nothing. To move a muscle the will must act upon the subconscious life that permeates that muscle; should it act upon the muscle itself, the muscle would become rigid, and muscular motion be made impossible.

No one can do anything by objectively willing to do it; he can do what he wants to do only by causing the will to act upon that part of the subconscious that can do what he wants to have done.

This law is absolute in all human actions, be they physical or metaphysical, intellectual or emotional, mental or spiritual.

To train the will to act only upon the subconscious, will increase the power of the conscious mind to impress the subconscious; the conscious action will not be divided, acting partly upon the objective and partly upon the subjective, but will give its power and attention absolutely to the idea that is being subconsciously impressed.

When the will acts only upon the subconscious, there will be no will force in the outer mind or body to disturb the normal functions of the systems; and when the entire system is normal the subconscious can readily do whatever it may be directed to do.

The conscious mind should employ the will solely for the purpose of impressing and directing the subconscious, but should give the subconscious unrestricted freedom to take full possession of the personality when expressions from within are expected to appear.

Those who hesitate to give the subconscious expressions full right of way, should remember that to move a muscle, the subconscious must take full possession of that muscle; and to think, the subconscious must exercise complete control of the mental faculty, and also, that the subconscious will only do what it is directed to do.

Though the personality must be controlled completely by the subconscious, the subconscious must be directed, in all its actions, by the conscious mind; therefore, the wide-awake self continues to be the master.

THE subconscious has the power to work out any problem, and find the exact answer to any question, at the time designated by the conscious mind; in fact, no problem is ever worked out by the conscious mind alone; the subconscious gives the real secret in every instance, though it is the conscious mind that makes the practical application.

To secure the direct and the fullest assistance from the subconscious when there are problems to solve, form a clear, distinct idea of what you wish to know, and impress that idea upon the subconscious with a deep, strong desire for the information required. Have perfect faith in the faith that you will receive the answer, and you will.

When you have something special to do at some near future time, that requires more power and mental brilliancy than you usually possess, direct the subconscious to give you the added power and intelligence at the exact time. The subconscious is exact as to time, and will produce, at the time desired, as much power and intelligence as you felt you needed for the special work when the impression was made.

To simply impress upon the subconscious a desire for more power is not sufficient; the impression must contain a clear idea of how much power is required and what the added power is expected to do.

While the subconscious is being impressed for more power, the mind must try to discern and feel the life of more power; and the amount of power that is discerned while the impression is being made, the subconscious will express at the time fixed for the expression.

Whenever an impression is made upon the subconscious, the conscious mind should try to gain the very highest and the very largest conception possible of the idea that is being impressed; and the more clearly the conscious mind discerns the largeness, the worth and the superiority of that idea, the larger, the worthier and the more superior will be the corresponding expression brought forth from the within.

When the conscious mind can see clearly the amount of power and mental brilliancy required for the special future action, and impresses that idea upon the subconscious with the deepest and the strongest desire for its realization, the impression thus made will call for the exact amount of power and intelligence required; and whatever the impression calls for the subconscious will supply.

The law is this, that the subconscious will respond with the exact quality and the exact quantity that you were conscious of, or that you can mentally discern and feel at the time the impression is being made. It is, therefore, extremely important to elevate the conscious mind into the largest and the most superior states of thought and feeling possible before an effort is made to impress the subconscious. In fact, this is the real secret in directing the subconscious to express a larger quantity and a higher quality than we ever received in tangible life before.

To live constantly in the deep, interior feeling of greater power, greater intelligence, greater personal worth and greater mental brilliancy, is to constantly call upon the subconscious to produce these things in larger and larger measure; and the subconscious will invariably do whatever it is called upon to do.

Though we should not live in the future in the sense that the mind dwells wholly in the thought of the future, nevertheless, we should always plan ahead.

Place your future plans in the hands of the subconscious; impress upon the subconscious what you wish to have done to-morrow, next week, next month, or even next year; then direct the great within to work out the best plans and the best methods possible, and to give your faculties the understanding and the power to carry out those plans to the most successful termination.

When there is something upon which you cannot decide, inform the subconscious that a definite decision is desired at such and such a time; impress clearly and deeply the facts on all sides concerned, and *know* that the great within can give the desired decision at the time stated.

When this time comes you will receive your answer through the feeling of a strong, irresistible desire to take one particular course, and that alone.

While the answer is being expected, no anxiety should be felt, even though the last minute should arrive before anything definite appears; the mind that continues in serenity and faith will receive the right answer before it is too late; but the anxious mind will, through the confusion produced by the anxiety, prevent the subconscious from giving expression to the desired information.

When two antagonistic decisions appear at the time fixed, the subconscious expression has not been given full right of way. One of these decisions will be of the conscious mind who judges according to appearances; the other will be of the sub-conscious who judges according to facts, but which is which may seem difficult to discern.

The decision of the conscious mind may sometimes be the stronger, but at other times the weaker; one's strongest feelings, therefore, at such times will not prove to be safe guidance.

To reimpress the subconscious for an immediate and a definite decision is the proper course to pursue under such circumstances, and if the conscious mind is kept quiet, in faith, the true answer will shortly appear. You will then feel a strong desire to take but one course, and will lose all desire to even think about the other, because when the subconscious action is given full and free expression, everything that is antagonistic to that expression will cease to exist.

It is therefore evident that we may completely eliminate the wrong by directing the subconscious to express the right, and by giving the subconscious absolute freedom to do what it has been directed to do.

HE subconscious should be called upon to give direct assistance in everything, even in the most insignificant of everyday affairs; this practice will not only cause all things to be done better and better constantly, but the conscious mind will be more thoroughly trained to impress the subconscious for anything desired, and the subconscious mentality will be perpetually enlarged along all lines.

To enlarge the subconscious mentality in every phase of interior action is to awaken a larger measure of the great within, and the more of the within that is awakened the greater will man become.

For these reasons the subconscious should be called upon for superior aid before anything, even the least, is undertaken. Everything that is worth doing should be done better than before, and the subconscious can provide the power.

Impressions of this nature should be made a few hours in advance, or, when possible, a few days in advance; though the subconscious can respond upon a moment's notice; its superior power should therefore be sought upon every occasion.

In the commercial world no one should

ever attempt to decide upon important transactions before directing the subconscious to inspire the mind with the highest insight, the keenest judgment, and the broadest understanding; and no great enterprise should be undertaken before directing the subconscious to work out the best possible plans and methods.

The subconscious can do these things, and when all practical men will go to the greater mind for their plans and ideas, instead of depending upon the limited intelligence of the lesser mind, failures will be reduced to a minimum, while great achievements will steadily increase, both in numbers and in greatness.

Those who are engaged in literary work will find the subconscious indispensable, because any idea desired may be gained from the great within.

Orators and public speakers should never attempt to prepare or deliver a discourse before going to this great source of ideas for their thought; and the same is true of musical composers, creative artists, inventors, and all others who require ideas that have originality and worth.

Every person who is engaged in study, or in any line of improvement, may increase results from ten to two hundred per cent by securing the direct assistance of the subconscious; and as all advancement and promotion in life comes directly from the improvement of self, the fact that the subconscious can supply any amount of ability, capacity and power, becomes extremely important.

All memory is subconscious, therefore, whatever one desires to remember should be deeply impressed upon the subconscious at the time the fact or idea is received; and the subconscious may be directed to bring back to mind these facts and ideas whenever their recollection is desired.

Through this simple process memory can be developed and cultivated to a remarkable degree, and the power to recall anything at any time will become practically perfect.

The subconscious can be trained to keep the conscious mind clear and active, and all sluggishness or obtuseness can be completely eliminated from every faculty. This will enable the student to learn with far greater rapidity, and every mental effort will be conducive to growth.

To produce these results the subconscious should, several times every day, be directed to express continuous clearness, mental lucidity, and a high, well-poised mental activity. While producing that impression, picture in the conscious mind the same clearness and action that you desire the subconscious to express.

To picture perfect lucidity, and to feel high activity in the conscious mind for a few moments while the subconscious is being impressed, will cause the subconscious to express that same clearness and activity for several hours; and when the impression contains a deep desire for greater clearness and activity than the conscious mind can discern, the greater clearness and activity will be expressed.

It is a well-known fact that nearly all great minds, and also most minds that are trying to develop greatness, have moods when they can do most excellent work, but when they are not in those moods little or nothing of worth can be accomplished. To such minds the ability to create the right moods, or mental states, whenever desired, would be of exceptional value, and by properly directing the subconscious it may readily be accomplished.

Form in the conscious mind a very clear idea of the mood or mental state in which you can do your best work, and impress that idea upon the subconscious with a strong desire for the continuous realization of the desired state. Repeat the impression several times every day, and every evening before going to sleep. Perseverance will produce the most remarkable results.

While engaged in any particular study,

impress frequently upon the subconscious the real nature of that study, and direct the subconscious to express all the essentials that may be necessary to thoroughly understand and master that study.

Expect superior intelligence from within, and make the best possible use of that intelligence as it is being received. Thus the conscious mind and the subconscious will work together for the promotion of the highest conceivable attainments.

To promote advancement in one's vocation, better plans and methods will constantly be in demand; and by directing the subconscious to work them out these may be secured as required; in addition, the necessary power and ability to practically apply those methods may also be secured if the subconscious is called upon to supply them.

It is the truth that whatever the subconscious is properly impressed and directed to do, it positively will do.

TO promote the highest development of mind and soul, a sunny disposition is indispensable; the brighter, the happier and the sweeter the disposition, the more easily and the more rapidly will any talent develop; and it is a literal truth that a sunny disposition is to the talents of the mind what a sunny day is to the flowers of the field.

Every form of disposition comes from the subconscious, be it sweet or otherwise; but the undesirable may be removed completely, and the sweetest and brightest disposition imaginable be permanently established, by daily impressing upon the subconscious your most perfect idea of a sweet and wholesome nature.

As the sweetness of human nature develops, all undesirable feelings and dispositions will disappear; no thought, therefore, should be given to the elimination of perverse characteristics, but the whole of attention should be concentrated upon the development of the wholesome, the sweet and the beautiful.

When there is a tendency to feel out of sorts, turn attention upon the finer side of your nature—the subconscious—and think deeply, strongly and feelingly of joy, brightness, kindness, amiableness, cheerfulness, sweetness and loveliness; try to enter into the very life of those states and *feel* that your entire nature is being recreated in the image and likeness of all that is sweet and beautiful.

To permit yourself to feel surly whenever there is a tendency to feel that way is to impress the subconscious with such a state of mind, and the subconscious will respond by giving your nature a stronger tendency to feel surly and out of sorts at the least provocation.

The first indication of ill-feeling in any shape or form should be counteracted at once by immediately directing the subconscious to give expression to the sweet, the wholesome and the beautiful.

It is not only the privilege of every mind to attain greatness, but no mind is doing justice to self that is not doing its utmost to develop greatness; and since a sunny disposition is absolutely necessary to the steady development of ability, talent and genius, neither time nor effort should be spared in recreating the subconscious so completely that every part of its vast domain is permeated through and through with the highest order of human sweetness and mental sunshine.

To recreate the subconscious mentality

in the likeness of higher ideals, every impression given to the subconscious should have *soul*. It is the conscious realization of soul that gives quality, worth and superiority to everything that appears in human life; the reason being that the soul *is* superiority, and that everything gains superiority that comes in conscious touch with the soul.

To feel *soul* is to feel the life of real worth, and to impress that feeling upon the subconscious will cause the subconscious to give real worth to every part of the personality.

The subconscious should be directed daily to give worth and superiority to the entire being of man; and this it positively can do.

The great within should be directed to work for greater things, and when every impression is impressed in the feeling of soul, every impression will cause the within to unfold, develop and give expression to greater things.

All greatness comes from the awakening of the great within; to awaken the great within is to feel greatness, and to be filled with the power that *is* greatness—the power that will invariably produce greatness.

Ability, talent and genius of the highest order must inevitably follow the development of the great within; likewise, the strong mind, the invincible character and the beautiful soul.

Every faculty increases in power, capacity and quality as its subconscious side is being developed, and this subconscious side may be developed by concentrating attention upon the interior, finer essence of that faculty while the most perfect idea or conception of that faculty is held in mind.

The development of the subconscious side of the entire personality will increase the drawing power of the personality, the power that attracts, both directly and indirectly, whatever the mind may desire.

This power is the result of subconscious action, and therefore increases, both in volume and in natural attraction, as a greater measure of the within is awakened.

There are many personalities that are strong, but that do not attract, while there are many others that lack in power but that are very attractive in proportion to the power they do possess. The cause of the former condition is an awakened subconscious life that does not receive free and orderly expression; the cause of the latter condition is a limited subconscious life that is not disturbed nor hindered in its expression.

To steadily increase subconscious action

and give that action a well-poised expression will cause the personality to become practically irresistible in its power of attraction.

The drawing power of the subconscious lies in its ability, not only to give extraordinary power to the personality, but also to produce ideas that draw, plans that draw, methods that draw and systems that draw.

It is not only ideas, but the way those ideas are arranged, that determines results; and it is not only high-class work, but the way that work is presented, that determines the measure of success. The best ideas may be ignored completely by the world, and the best work may have to be abandoned through the lack of appreciation, and the subconscious life that is expressed through those ideas or efforts is at fault.

Direct the subconscious not only to give you the best ideas, the best plans and the best methods, but also direct the subconscious to give the proper expression to those ideas and methods. When the proper expression is made the attention of the world will be attracted; your ideas will be understood, the real worth of your work will be appreciated, and your efforts will be in constant demand.

The subconscious can work out the best ideas and create the best expression of those ideas; it can give the power and the ability to do greater things, and can give your work that mysterious something that will attract both the attention and the appreciation of the world.

The subconscious in every mind should therefore be directed to do these things, because no person is just to himself who does not make the best use of everything that exists in his nature.

The subconscious, when so directed, will give a natural drawing power to all the finer thought currents; these in turn will convey the same qualities to every part of the mentality and the personality; this will cause everything that man is, and everything that he does, to be stamped with that something that attracts attention and commands appreciation; his desires will consequently become irresistible.

The desires of such a mind will have the power to create their own way to their own goal, no matter how lofty that goal may be. The power of the subconscious is limitless, therefore, nothing becomes impossible when we awaken the great within.

All desires should be made subconscious, and when those desires are constantly expressed with the deepest feeling and the strongest desire that can possibly be aroused, you will positively receive what you want. If it fails to come through one channel it will come through another; but come it will, because the subconscious has the power to do whatever it is directed to do.

To subconsciously desire something is to make yourself strong enough and able enough to command, create or attract that something.

Make your desires subconscious and the subconscious will make you worthy of what you desire; the subconscious desire will awaken the same quality and worth in yourself that already exists in that which you desire, and, as like does attract like, you will invariably get what you desire when you become equal to what you desire.

The subconscious desire for abundance will develop in yourself the power to earn and create abundance; it will increase your earning capacity, and will, both directly and indirectly, change your personality so that you will be naturally drawn into environments and associations where you can make the best possible use of that increase of capacity.

The subconscious, being limitless, can work out ideas and plans that you can use in your present position in furthering your desire for the better position; the subconscious, if directed, will find a way; especially so if the desire is very deep and very strong; and you will also receive the power and the ability to do whatever that way may demand.

It is therefore evident that whatever a person's conditions or circumstances may be to-day, the subconscious can, and will, open the door to something better, providing there is a strong subconscious desire for something better.

T O awaken the great within is to awaken to a universe of higher attainments, greater achievements and more far-reaching possibilities than one has ever dreamed of before; it is to enter that world where every desire will be granted, every aspiration realized and every ideal fulfilled.

To promote this awakening, direct the subconscious to give its best to every thought and every action, and when this best has been received, direct the subconscious to produce something still better. It can; the subconscious can do whatever we may wish to have done.

Every condition that appears in the body, be it favorable or otherwise, comes either directly or indirectly from the subconscious; that is, it may be the direct effect of a corresponding subconscious cause, or it may be the effect of external causes that were permitted to act upon the body because the true subconscious expression was absent.

No external cause can produce disease in the body so long as the subconscious is giving a full expression to perfect health; and no curative agent from the without can restore health in the body so long as the subconscious is giving expression to diseased conditions.

The majority of physical ills can be cured by nature when the subconscious ceases to give expression to weakening and disease-producing conditions, and all diseases can be permanently removed by training the subconscious to give a full and constant expression of health.

Personal and physical conditions are effects; they are caused either directly or indirectly by the subconscious; therefore, any condition desired in the personality may be produced through the proper direction of the subconscious.

To direct the subconscious to produce perfect health, the first essential is to gain a clear conscious realization of the state of perfect health, and the second essential is to permeate the subconscious with this realization.

The subconscious mind is a deeper and a finer state of mental life that exists within every atom of the human system; it is another mental world, so to speak, and is so immense that the ordinary conscious mind is mere insignificance in comparison. But it obeys perfectly the directions of the conscious mind, and, having limitless power in every part of the body, can readily banish any disease when properly directed to do so.

To impress the subconscious, attention should be concentrated upon this superior mental world, and all thought should be gradually refined until one can feel that the conscious thought has been completely transformed into the spiritual fineness of the subconscious thought.

The subconscious may be reached most directly by concentrating upon the brain center, though attention must not be fixed upon the physical brain, but upon that finer mental life that permeates the physical brain.

All general directions given to the subconscious should be given through the brain center, but for the curing of physical ailments attention should be concentrated upon the subconscious mentality that permeates the organ, muscle or nerve where the ailment is located.

To impress the conscious realization of health upon the subconscious life of any part of the body will cause the subconscious to bring forth into that part of the body the same condition of health which the conscious mind realized while the impression was being made; it is, therefore, necessary to attain the very highest possible conscious understanding of the real state of perfect health before the subconscious is directed to produce health.

No thought of disease should form in mind while the subconscious is being impressed with perfect health; neither should one think of the body. To think of the body is to form mental conceptions of the way physical conditions now feel, and if these conditions are undesirable, undesirable impressions will enter the subconscious, to be followed by the formation of more undesirable conditions in the near future.

The imperfection of physical conditions should never enter mind at any time, because such conditions are liable to be deeply felt, and whatever is deeply felt will be impressed upon the subconscious, whether we so wish or no; neither should there be any desire to remove or overcome that which may seem undesirable. To desire to remove the wrong is to deeply think about the wrong, because all desires tend to deepen the actions of thought, and to deeply think about the wrong is to impress the wrong upon the subconscious. It is sowing weeds in the fields of the mind, and the harvest will be accordingly.

All thought should be animated with the consciousness of that perfection in health and wholeness that we desire to realize in expression, and all feeling should be trained to feel the health, the life and the harmony that the subconscious is being directed to produce.

To consciously live through and through the finer subconscious mentality for a few moments, several times every day, and deeply impress one's most perfect realization of health upon the entire subconscious mentality will cause the subconscious to give a full and constant expression of health.

The result will be perpetual health, without a moment of any form of sickness at any time, and if the conscious mind will seek to daily impress upon the subconscious a more and more perfect realization of absolute health, the subconscious will steadily improve the quality of the health that is being expressed.

To eliminate a local ailment the subconscious mentality that permeates that part of the body should be impressed with the conscious feeling of the health that is desired.

Concentrate upon the finer mental life in that part of the body where the adverse condition appears and *feel* the reality of perfect health. Do not concentrate upon the physical organ, nor even think of the physical organ, but enter mentally into the interior subconscious life of that organ and, while in that state, *feel* the spirit of perfect health with all the depth of mind and soul.

What you feel, while in that state, you impress upon the subconscious, and the subconscious will cause perfect health to be expressed through every atom of that organ.

To eliminate a chronic ailment, impress perfect health upon the subconscious as a whole, while concentrating upon the subconscious mentality within the brain center. Also concentrate frequently upon the subconscious side of the entire personality, feeling the state of perfect health in the subconscious life of every part of the system.

If certain parts of the body are specially affected, impress those parts in the same way as for a local ailment, though local attention should be given, not so much to those parts of the body that feel the effects of the ailment as to those parts where the adverse condition has its origin.

Before impressing the subconscious the entire system should be made as calm and peaceful as possible, and the principal directions should be given to the subconscious immediately before going to sleep.

The most important of all, however, is to live, think and act in the absolute faith that the subconscious *can* and *will* do whatever it is directed to do.

URING the waking state the conscious ego acts directly upon the conscious, or wide-awake mind, while during sleep it acts entirely in the subconscious.

When we go to sleep all the principal thoughts, desires, intentions, tendencies, feelings and ideas that have formed during the day are taken into the subconscious, unless we eliminate the undesirable mental material before we permit sleep to take place.

Every thought, desire or idea that is taken into the subconscious as mind falls asleep will be impressed upon the subconscious, and will cause corresponding expressions to be brought forth into the personality. To eliminate all undesirable thoughts and feelings from mind before going to sleep is therefore extremely important.

Before going to sleep the conscious mind should be thoroughly cleansed from everything that one does not care to reproduce or perpetuate, and the subconscious should be given definite directions as to what should be developed, reproduced and expressed.

The hours of sleep may be employed in the development of anything we may have in view, because whatever we impress upon mind when we go to sleep will enter the subconscious and will cause the within to give expression to those effects that we desire to secure in the without.

Before going to sleep the subconscious should be given full directions as to what is to be done in the near future, and the exact time for each particular action should be specified as far as possible. In the meantime the subconscious will work out the best plans, methods and ideas, and provide the added understanding, insight and power required to apply those plans in the most effective manner.

When the subconscious is properly directed in this way the results from future actions may be increased to a degree that will frequently be remarkable, and, as much produces more, these results will follow the law of perpetual increase.

During the waking state the mind forms a definite conception of everything that is given real, conscious attention; these conceptions individualize themselves into ideas and as mind goes to sleep all those ideas are taken into the subconscious.

Therefore, what the subconscious is given to work out and develop during sleep will depend upon what we think about

during the day, and what we give the subconscious to develop and express will
determine what character, mentality and
personality are to be.

The subconscious makes us what we
are, in every respect, but what the subconscious is to make will depend upon what
our thoughts, feelings and desires may
direct.

The more we think during the day,
providing our thought has quality, the
more good seeds we shall place in the
garden of the mind during sleep, and the
greater will be the quality and the quantity
of the coming harvest.

The stronger our desires for wisdom,
power, attainments and achievements during the waking state, the more thoroughly
will the subconscious work for those things
during sleep.

The subconscious can provide all the
essentials required for the highest attainments and greatest achievements and will
do so if directed.

The subconscious works during sleep,
and works to develop the ideas and the
desires that the conscious mind brought
into the subconscious while falling asleep,
but the subconscious will give the same
attention to ideas and desires that are
detrimental, just as rich soil will apply the

same productiveness to the weed as to the flower.

It is therefore wisdom to sow good seeds only; to eliminate all undesirable thought, ideas and feelings before sleep begins.

The habit of going to sleep every night with all sorts of thoughts in mind is the principal cause of the continuous mingling of good and evil in the life of the average person. The troubles and the worries of the day are taken into the subconscious at night, along with those thoughts and feelings that have better things in view, and the subconscious, consequently, continues to work for more good things on the one hand and for more troubles and worries on the other.

It is the truth that any person may emancipate himself completely from all the ills of perverted life by refusing absolutely to permit a single undesirable thought, feeling or desire to enter the subconscious.

To prevent the wrong from entering the subconscious we must, during the waking state, never think, with feeling, of that which is evil, imperfect or wrong, and before going to sleep the conscious mind must be cleansed completely from every undesirable thought or impression that may have entered unconsciously during the day.

The imperfect will not impress itself upon the subconscious during the waking state unless we think about it in deep feeling, but everything that is in the conscious mind when we go to sleep will enter the subconscious and produce fruit after its kind.

To cleanse the conscious mind before going to sleep, enter a state of perfect mental poise; be still in the deepest sense of the term; forget what you do not wish to retain by entering into the very life and essence of that which you desire to awaken, unfold and develop. Then concentrate upon the subconscious with the deepest possible feeling and the strongest possible desire.

What you wish to remove from mind may be removed by directing the subconscious to create and express the opposite, though no thought should be given to that which is not to be retained. When you know what you wish to remove, forget it by giving your entire subconscious attention to that which you wish to create and realize instead.

To carry into the subconscious those ideas that we wish to develop is not all that is necessary, however, as we go to sleep; the subconscious should be given the best possible conditions in which to work.

The subconscious is in close touch with

all the functions of the body as well as the actions of the mind, therefore, the entire system must be in harmony and order before sleep begins or subconscious action will be confused and misdirected.

Before going to sleep the body should be in harmony, the mind in peace and the entire personality relaxed. The circulation should be even, and no part should be too warm nor too cold. Digestion should be practically finished and there should be nothing in the system that might disturb any of the functions during sleep.

When physical functions are disturbed during sleep the conscious ego is drawn back to the outer mind, either fully or in part, and its work in the subconscious is interrupted. Such interruptions usually misdirect the subconscious actions to such an extent that the very opposite results to what were intended are produced.

This explains why such detrimental results are frequently secured, even when our intentions were the best and our plans carried out with the greatest of care. It also proves that the entire system must be kept in order if every action, conscious or subconscious, is to produce the results desired.

HEN the conscious ego, which is you, yourself, enters the subconscious during s l e e p , there are two objects in view. The first object is to carry into the subconscious the new ideas that have formed during the day and the second object is to recharge the system with life, power and energy.

The subconscious supplies the life and the energy that is required to perpetuate the existence of the mentality and the personality, but to receive this energy the conscious ego must enter the subconscious, and should remain there, uninterruptedly, for six or seven hours out of every twenty-four, to secure the full measure of power.

When sleep is interrupted the personality does not receive as much life as may be required to keep the system in the fullest and most perfect action; personal efforts will, therefore, become inferior.

When all the conditions are provided for properly recuperating and recharging the system during sleep, and the subconscious is directed to steadily increase the supply of power, the personality will become stronger and more vigorous from year to year; instead of going down to weakness and age the personality will go on to greater strength, greater capacity, greater ability and greater power the longer you live.

To go to sleep properly is to wake up feeling refreshed, but to go to sleep with all sorts of impressions in the mind and all sorts of conditions in the body is to wake up feeling stupid and depressed.

To enter the subconscious with adverse impressions is to return to consciousness with similar conditions. Like causes always produce like effects.

To aid the mind in purifying itself before going to sleep, attention should be concentrated upon the purest purity and the highest worth that can possibly be imagined, and to place the entire system in a state of peace, concentrate the thought of peace upon the brain center while gently drawing all the finer forces of mind toward that center.

To think, with feeling, of the finer forces of mind during this process will produce immediate results.

The practice of "sleeping over" difficult problems before definite decisions are made is a practice of great value, especially when the subconscious is properly directed in the matter, because the subconscious can "turn things over" more completely during sleep than during the waking state.

To secure the best results hold clearly and serenely in mind the elements involved in the problem just as you are going to sleep and desire deeply, but without anxiety, to receive the correct answer upon awakening.

The higher and the clearer the conception that is formed of the problem during the waking state the more readily can the subconscious work it out during sleep. The same is true in the various ideas that are formed during the day and that are taken into the great within either at sleep or during waking states of deep feeling.

It is therefore extremely important to form the highest possible conception of everything that we think of during the day, and whatever attracts our attention should be considered from the very highest point of view.

Live in the upper story of mind and give *soul* to all your thought; you will thereby form ideas with real quality and worth, and as those ideas are taken into the subconscious during sleep they will cause greater quality and worth to be developed in you.

No person can afford to take a commonplace view of anything, nor to indulge in cheap thinking at any time; to do so is to place inferior seeds in the garden of the mind.

There are days when the average person feels as if he amounted to practically nothing; his personality lacks energy and his mind is dull, stupid and confused. Cheap, superficial thinking a day or two before is the cause.

Give inferior ideas to the subconscious, and the subconscious will, in the near future, not only cause you to feel incompetent and inferior, but your mind will temporarily be placed in a state where it actually becomes incompetent and inferior.

To produce worthy ideas it is not necessary to always continue in profound or serious states of mind; the thought of worth is the thought that mind creates while attention dwells in the life of quality and soul, and while consciousness is thoroughly permeated with the desire to realize quality and soul in everything.

Such thinking can be taken into all thought and all life, even into every pleasure.

To try to enjoy pleasures while mind skims over the surface of life and thought is to fail to receive the joy that is joy, or the satisfaction that does satisfy; but when pleasures are entered into with the feeling of quality and finer life, even the simplest of joys become founts of supreme joy.

Everything that we thoroughly enjoy we impress upon the subconscious; therefore, to enter into pleasure while mind is in the attitude of cheapness or inferiority is a mistake to be avoided under every circumstance.

However, our pleasures may be used as channels through which the subconscious may be impressed and directed along lines of superior attainment, and pleasures that are employed in this manner will invariably give the greatest, the most satisfying and the most wholesome joy of all joys.

HE entire human personality is being constantly renewed; there is nothing about mind or body that can possibly become old, except the appearance, and the appearance of age is caused by a wrong subconscious process.

The process of perpetual renewal is carried on by the subconscious, but it is what the conscious mind gives to the subconscious that determines both the quality and the appearance of the personality.

To constantly give the subconscious better ideas, better desires, better thoughts and better mental states is to cause the improvement of character, mentality and personality to become perpetual.

To provide better material for the subconscious, the conscious mind, before going to sleep, should eliminate everything but those ideas, thoughts and desires that have quality and worth, and every effort should be made during the waking state to form the most superior ideas possible on every subject with which the mind may come in contact.

Never go to sleep discouraged, nor with the thought of failure in mind. To fear failure while going to sleep is to impress the subconscious with the idea of failure, and the subconscious will respond by producing conditions in the system that are failures; the system will, consequently, fail to be its best, and will lose ground, more and more, until real failure takes place.

To go to sleep discouraged, disappointed, worried or depressed, is to impress the subconscious with weakening tendencies; these will cause the subconscious to express conditions of weakness in every faculty and in every part of mind or body.

The tendency downward in any career originates invariably in depressed subconscious states, the majority of which are taken into the subconscious as the mind goes to sleep.

Every tendency upward and onward toward higher attainments and greater achievements, originates in constructive subconscious states and it is possible for anyone to produce such states at will.

By going to sleep with strong, clear ideas of health, harmony, power, advancement and success, clearly held in mind, the causes of those things will be formed in the subconscious and the effects will invariably appear in external life. Your health will at once begin to improve; more power will appear in mind and body; capacity will increase; all your talents and faculties will be filled with the spirit of success, and will consequently, do far better work than ever before.

To continue, for weeks and months, the practice of giving superior ideas of all kinds to the subconscious, upon going to sleep, will cause the character, the mentality and the personality to improve to such an extent that, in comparison with your former self, you will actually become a superior being.

When the subconscious is given something special to do every night sleep will become more restful; the subconscious always works during sleep, but will work more orderly when given something definite to do.

After the subconscious has been properly directed no anxiety should be felt as to results; perfect faith in the law, with that quiet assurance that knows, will give the law the proper conditions through which the desired results can be produced.

When we go to sleep in states of discord the mental material becomes confused and incoherent mental formations are produced; these are sometimes remembered as disagreeable dreams.

All such formations are produced by confusion among the subconscious creative energies and indicate that the true state of sleep was not entered completely, also that the subconscious was not properly impressed the night before.

Orderly and coherent dreams may indicate what tendencies are at work in the subconscious and whether desirable or undesirable conditions are being formed, because a dream is always a partial memory of what is taking place in the subconscious.

By noting this fact, undesirable conditions may be counteracted and removed before they advance sufficiently to produce tangible results.

An undesirable dream should always be counteracted at once by impressing the opposite, desirable conditions and qualities upon the subconscious; tendencies, however, that are indicated in good dreams, should be given added power. This can be done by directing the subconscious to work more thoroughly for the promotion of the greater good at hand.

Every good dream is a prophecy; that is, it indicates what the subconscious can do, what it is ready to do, or what it is about to do along certain lines, and this prophecy can be made to come true by directing the subconscious to proceed along those lines with greater power and determination than ever before.

These directions should be given to the subconscious as frequently as possible during the waking state, as well as before going to sleep.

Every desirable indication among the greater, interior life forces, whether it be discovered through dreams or intuition, should be taken advantage of at once, and all the forces of mind should be concentrated upon the goal that the vision has placed within reach; a successful termination will invariably be the result; the dream will come true, the prophecy will be fulfilled, the ideal will be realized.

THE subconscious mind is not a second mind; to think so is to place an artificial barrier between the outer person and the limitless within. There is but one mind; the outer phase is the conscious or the objective; the inner phase is the subconscious or the subjective.

The subconscious is within the conscious, and, being unlimited, both in power and in possibilities, is appropriately termed the great within.

To awaken the great within is to bring into action the powers and the possibilities that are latent in the subconscious, and since the powers of the within are limitless, and its possibilities numberless, this awakening may be promoted indefinitely, increasing without end the worth and the greatness of man.

The awakening of the great within is promoted directly through a perpetual increase of conscious action upon the subconscious, and the power of the conscious mind to act upon the subconscious will increase in proportion to the practical use that is made of every added expression that appears from the within.

The fact that the within is limitless, and

the fact that the greatness of the within can be brought forth into expression in greater and greater measure through the proper action of the conscious mind upon the subconscious proves conclusively that man may become as great as he may desire to be, and that his ability, his talent and his genius may be developed, not only to a most remarkable degree, but to any degree.

Personally, each person is only as much as he has, consciously or unconsciously, directed the subconscious to produce, and he will remain what he is so long as he does not direct the subconscious to produce more; but he may become more, as much more as his highest aspiration can picture, by awakening the great within.

To train the conscious mind to act upon the subconscious with the greatest efficiency, a clear idea of how the two phases of mind are related to each other becomes necessary, and this idea is readily understood when we realize that mind is an immense sea of soul forces, all of which move in circles and spirals.

The circumference of each circle is acted upon by the conscious ego during the waking state, therefore, the sum total of all the circumferences of all the mental circles may be termed the outer mind, the objective mind, the conscious mind, the wide-awake mind.

During sleep the conscious ego withdraws from the circumference of the mental circles and enters the mental field within; that is, the subconscious.

While the mind is in a state of deep feeling the conscious ego acts partly upon the conscious side of mind and partly upon the subconscious; it is possible, therefore, while in that state, to impress upon the subconscious what we think or feel in the conscious.

To secure the best and the largest results from every mental action the conscious ego should, during the waking state, act constantly both upon the conscious and the subconscious. To be in constant touch with the limitless powers of the within will add remarkably to the capacity as well as the quality of the faculties that may be in use, and every conscious desire will enter the subconscious at once, so that an immediate response may be secured, if required.

The strong mind is the mind that is in such close touch with the great within that the limitless powers of the within can be felt at any time.

The capacity of such a mind will be practically unbounded; weariness will be absent; mental brilliancy will ever be on the increase, and instead of going down with the years, as the average mind does, such a mind will steadily advance in higher attainments and greater achievements the longer the person may live.

The mind that has presence of mind at all times, and under all circumstances, is in perfect touch with the subconscious. In fact, if the subconscious is impressed every day, or better still, several times a day, to guide the outer mind so perfectly that the right step will always be taken at the right time, the conscious mind will intuitively know what to do to secure the best results from every circumstance, action or event.

When the powers of the subconscious are realized one's ideas will become much higher than before, and there will be a tendency to form ideals that cannot be realized with present states of development, but since the proper direction of the subconscious can promote development to any degree desired, it is not justice to self to remain content with the lesser while the greater is in view.

However, no desire should be entertained that cannot be fulfilled through the complete application of present ability, nor should present demands go beyond what present capacity is known to be..

The proper course is to first increase

the capacity, then desire what the increased capacity has the power to fulfill.

The small mind must not desire the realization of ideals that the great mind alone can possibly make real; such a course would be a waste of time; it would be schooling oneself to desire only what cannot be secured, while doing nothing to so increase one's power that the object in view could easily be secured.

The subconscious can make the small mind great, as great as may be necessary to realize any ideal, but greatness does not come from dreaming about the ideal, nor from concentrating upon that which is beyond our present capacity to produce.

Develop greatness by awakening the great within, and that power that can produce anything and realize anything will be gained.

Development is gradual and does not simply consist in the unfoldment of added power and capacity, but also in the full tangible use of that power and capacity.

To proceed orderly toward greatness direct the subconscious to express what may be necessary to take the next step forward; concentrate all the forces of mind upon that step, and do not scatter mind over realms and spheres that are beyond that step; do now what you are doing now, and be satisfied to realize what can be realized now.

Proceed with the second step in the same way and, likewise, with the innumerable steps that are to follow.

This is true progress; it is concentrating the whole of attention upon the present advancement, and there is no other advancement. To move forward we must advance in the present, and in the present only.

To move forward now is the purpose, and he who continues to move forward now will reach any goal he may have in view.

The subconscious should, therefore, be directed to turn all its superior powers upon the present forward movement and should be daily impressed to desire, not the ideals of the distant future, but the ideals that can be realized to-day.

This forward movement, however, should not be confined to any one phase of existence; all things in the physical, the metaphysical and the spiritual nature of man should be developed simultaneously and perpetually.

It is the greatness of everything in man that gives man the greatness that *is* greatness, and the perpetual awakening of the great within will produce this greatness, because to the powers and the possibilities of the great within there is no limit, neither is there any end.